Cristina Flores

Guilt, Empathy and Reason: How Photojournalism Supported the Civil Rights Movement

GRIN Verlag

Bibliografische Information der Deutschen Nationalbibliothek:

Die Deutsche Bibliothek verzeichnet diese Publikation in der Deutschen National-
bibliografie; detaillierte bibliografische Daten sind im Internet über http://dnb.d-
nb.de/ abrufbar.

Imprint:

Copyright © 2013 GRIN Verlag GmbH
Druck und Bindung: Books on Demand GmbH, Norderstedt Germany
ISBN: 978-3-656-61891-1

This book at GRIN:

http://www.grin.com/en/e-book/270526/guilt-empathy-and-reason-how-photojour-
nalism-supported-the-civil-rights

University of Paderborn

Faculty of Cultural Sciences

Institute of English and American Studies

Seminar: Photography and the American Culture

Guilt, Empathy and Reason :

How Photojournalism Supported the Civil Rights Movement

Name: Cristina dSF

Course of study: Lehramt GyGe English/French

Semester: 8

Table of Contents

1.   Introduction: The Civil Rights Movement

The African American Civil Rights Movement of the 1950s and 1960s can be seen as one of the major events in America's history that fundamentally changed its entire society. In one of the most liberal countries in the world that defeated fascism and fought against communism, people of different ethnicity were still treated differently. While white people enjoyed all the rights, black people were excluded from public places, did not have the right to vote and were punished more severely than their fellow citizens. But the African American population stood up against these kinds of suppression and segregation in the middle of the 20th century and fought for their rights, especially with the help of their leading figures such as Martin Luther King Jr., Rosa Parks and Malcolm X. Even if they could eventually achieve some of their goals such as the abolition of segregated buses or the right to vote, their peaceful movement was most of the times violently stopped by policemen and white civilians.

Due to this unequal fight, the blacks' demands and sufferings captured more and more the media's attention and were documented especially through photography. This photography had a high impact on how the Civil Rights Movement was perceived all over the country and, as a consequence, indirectly helped the protestors in their plans. Interestingly enough, it is remarkable that nearly all these printed photographs show the Movement in a way that was unknown to people so that special emotions towards black people and the own behaviors were evoked: empathy and guilt. This then led to a new debate about racial discrimination and civil rights.

In this term paper I will therefore examine in more detail in which way photojournalism supported the African American Civil Rights Movement. I will start by giving a short overview of photojournalism and its effects on society. Then, I will continue by analyzing different types of photographs of the Civil Rights Movement that evoke feelings of empathy and guilt. For this purpose I will describe one exemplary photograph for each category and explain how influenced society. Finally, a conclusion with possibilities to expand the topic will follow.

2.   Photojournalism and Its Effect on the Society of the 1950s and 1960s

Photojournalism can be described as "the work of giving news using mainly photographs" ("photojournalism", *Oxford Advanced Learner's Dictionary*). Its success started in the middle of the 20th century thanks to the invention of smaller cameras which were easier to transport and to handle in comparison to cameras of earlier times. While in the beginning of the 20th century news were mainly transported by text in combination with some photographs all taken in the same style due to its difficult operation, newer cameras allowed the photographs to take more individual photographs. Journalists were now given the opportunity to not only take one picture for the sake of a specific article but to construct a whole report or study on a chosen topic or event which could then published, for example in a magazine. (Lemagny/Rouillé 166)

One of the first magazines showing pictorial journalism was *Life Magazine,* founded in 1936. According to its founder Henry Luce the magazine's aim, which is still up-to-date, was

> [t]o see life; to see the world; to eyewitness great events; to watch the faces of the poor and the gestures of the proud; to see strange things — machines, armies, multitudes, shadows in the jungle and on the moon; to see man's work — his paintings, towers and discoveries; to see things thousands of miles away, things hidden behind walls and within rooms, things dangerous to come to; the women that men love and many children; to see and take pleasure in seeing; to see and be amazed; to see and be instructed...(Smith 342)

The strongest motivation for photojournalists was and is therefore "the belief [that] their pictures can make life better for their fellow humans" (Cookman 139). Through photojournalism people are given the opportunity to gain knowledge about events and to re-experience them thanks to the subject who is shown in a significant moment of his life. The viewer is then sees what the subject is feeling and develops own feelings for the situation shown. Karen Slattery summarizes it by stating that only "excellent photographs convey [both], the emotion of the subject [and] and emotion in the viewer" (Slattery/Doremus). The photographs which are going to be analyzed in the next chapters belong to this category of "excellence" with reference to the Civil Rights Movement.

Due to these emotions transported through photography, photojournalism is able to change society. Emotional photographs in journals or magazines are able to provoke discussions and controversies, not only between private persons but in politics, especially if a country's principles are affected by these photographs and if feelings of empathy and guilt are evoked. This was the case as far as the Civil Rights Movement was concerned: The population and home and abroad sympathized with these clear, persuasive and powerful photographs and, seeing the blacks' struggle, demanded some sort of change. The United States then obviously feared of losing their wanted image as a country of democracy and had to react, for example by cooperating with demonstrators and changing laws. (cf. Kasher 8)

Meaningful photographs taken by photojournalists and telling the story of a specific important event therefore definitely generate publicity and can change society. During the 1950s and 1960s "scenes unthinkable to Americans as American were shown to American and the world [so that] public sympathy and financial support, as well as political backing, flowed to movement organizations." (8)

3. Photographs Evoking Empathy

Empathy is a person's "ability to understand the emotions that other feel in response to circumstances and situations. It involves putting ourselves in the place of 'the other'." (Slattery/Doremus) As already explained, this feeling is in particular important for photography since it makes the viewer sympathize with the subject and his or her personal situation. During the African American Civil Rights Movement this empathy towards the blacks was mainly evoked through portraits and photographs showing the everyday life. These two types of photography show the subject in very personal and authentic moments which make especially the 'superior' whites rethink their opinion about their black fellow citizens and finally realize that they actually are the same and have the right to be treated equally.

3.1. Portraits

Especially in the 20th century portraits are of major importance as, thanks to technology, photographers can "capture the expression of the subject as it might appear in the flash of an instant, not just an 'average' or typical facial mask." (Ovell 35) The subject therefore does not have to be prepared but also can be photographed in an accidental moment. These portraits are then more authentic than posed ones as they mainly have the aim to present the subject in a certain manner. That is why portraits by photojournalist more often show sudden moments with more significant facial expressions that, as a consequence, are able to evoke stronger emotions.

In the 1960s a powerful portrait was taken, for example, during the Selma-to-Montgomery march in March 1965 by Bruce Davidson (Fig. 1). About 3000 people joined this march which was led by Martin Luther King and aimed to dramatize the need for a federal voter registration law. (cf. Dierenfield 117) Davidson's photograph shows a young black marcher with conspicuous suncream on his face in front of other marchers and the American flag. On his forehead he inscribed the word "vote" and also his mouth is formed as if he was saying this word while this snapshot was taken. Due to the fact that portraits concentrate on the subject's face, this portrait is especially interesting as the marcher's face is in some way manipulated in order to transport more meaning to the public than his natural face would do among all the other marchers. With the suncream on his face he wants to convey the message that skin color does not make a person an inferior one. If his skin was white he would have the right to vote but because he is black this wish is denied. His eyes clearly demonstrate his determination and will to achieve some progress in terms of rights for his generation living in the United States. Every portrait therefore tells a story. In this case it is the story of a young black who feels like an American, which can be seen in the holding of the flag, but is not treated like other, white Americans. The effort the young man puts into the march evokes empathy in the viewer. Due to the suncream the viewer realizes that if the young man had the choice he would prefer being white, only because they are allowed to vote. It is then very likely that the white viewer, in particular, detects the arbitrariness of racial segregation.

In the media, this peaceful and nonviolent march was followed very actively. After hearing about violent attempts by segregationists to stop the march "thousands of white and black Americans flooded into the White House with telegrams, signed petitions, and demonstrated [...] to end the violence" (118). Owing to news report even "the president [Lyndon B. Johnson] considered the Selma protest a turning point in American history" (120) and supported it by signing the Voting Rights Act in August 1965.

The media therefore highly supported the Civil Rights Movement though the reporting about this topic. As far as photography is concerned, especially portraits made people look closer into what happened on the streets, as faces are able to transport emotions very powerfully. This power evoked empathy and made the population become committed in helping the blacks.

3.2. The Everyday Life

Apart from portraits it was also photography showing the everyday life which influenced the American people and thus, indirectly, supported the Civil Rights Movement. In general, "everyday life is considered to be what most characterizes 'reality'" (Tormey 54) since the word 'everyday' implies the idea of continuity, authenticity and comfort. If people are photographed in every life activities they normally feel sure in what they are doing as it is a usual activity. This also means that these photographs are snapshots during an activity so that the subjects seem to be not aware of being photographed. What is presented apart from the subject such as the place or objects are as important as the subject itself. Due to the fact that white people did not often have the opportunity to photograph black in their daily life, a new group of black photographers developed with the aim to "represent black people as other than a social problem for a white audience" (Roberts 120). Feelings of empathy are then evoked since white people gain an authentic insight in the life of black people and are then able to compare it to their own way of life. The aim of this type of photography is therefore to make the white population realize that whites share a lot of similarities in every part of the daily life with their black fellow citizens and, therefore, should enjoy the same rights.

This everyday life was, above others, photographed by the black photographer Gordon Parks who illustrated a reporting about black families in *Life Magazine*. What makes these everyday photographs evoke empathy is that "most of the images are optimistic and affirmative. [...] They focus on the family's everyday activities, and their resolve to get on with their lives as normally as possible, in spite of an environment that restricts and intimidates." (Berger) One photograph shows, for example, black children in front of the fence of a playground (Fig. 2). The article's author Robert Wallace additionally explains that

> "[the Tanner family] must tell their children, for example, that they cannot play in a nearby playground for whites but must use a 'separate but equal' one for Negroes. The children do not grasp the logic of this and view the white playground as a special, wonderful place from which they are deliberately excluded" (106)

This image is especially powerful because children are involved. The viewer automatically feels pity for them as their wish to play with other children is not fulfilled. Finally, also this photograph indirectly supported the Civil Rights Movement. The Civil Right Act of 1964 "banned discrimination in such places of public accommodations. [...] It authorized the attorney general to bring an end to segregation in public schools, hospitals, libraries, and playgrounds". (166)

4.   Photographs Evoking Guilt

Guilt, the "feeling of anxiety or unhappiness [after having] done something immoral or wrong, such as causing harm to another person" ("guilt", *Oxford Advanced Learner's Dictionary*) does not necessarily mean that one has to be the one causing harm. It can also mean that one feels guilty because another person of the same group does something wrong. This is the case looking at the Civil Rights Movement. Many photographs, especially sign photography and photographs of street fights, show a wrong behavior towards blacks, whether directly through violence or indirectly through racial segregation laws. Even if the white viewer of these photographs cannot be blamed for the misbehavior of the persons responsible, feelings of guilt are evoked since it appears as if the segregationists' opinion fits to the opinion of all white citizens in general. As this assumption is obviously incorrect, photographs evoking guilt also made the whites support the blacks' movement.

4.1. Sign Photography

Sign photography during the Civil Rights Movement implies all kinds of signs on photographs dealing with segregation orders that were laid down in the so-called Jim Crow Laws: "From 1881 to 1964, Jim Crow Laws separated Americans by race. […] In most American cities, towns, and States, North and South people lived in segregated neighborhoods and attended schools that were all white or all black." (Tischauser xi) Signs were then used to separate nearly all parts of the everyday life, such as busses, restaurants or drinking fountains and accepted in public. But the publication of this type of photography changed the perception of these sign photographs as the variety of these images made the public realize the arbitrariness and "mutable construction" (Abel 146) of Jim Crow.

Elliott Erwitt was one of the photographers who concentrated on segregation photography, for example by photographing segregated water fountains (Fig. 3). One of these photographs shows a black man drinking out of a public water fountain with the inscription 'coloured'. On the other side, there is another, bigger and cleaner water fountain with the inscription 'white'. What makes this photograph arbitrary is that even if both fountains are next to each other and probably give the same water, black people are forced to use a special fountain due to their skin color. Moreover, only because of the way the basin looks it seems as if the whites' water is of better quality as the black man is looking at it while drinking. The photograph clearly demonstrates the injustice and discrimination against black people which is obvious for everyone who looks at this image. Feelings of guilt are therefore evoked in the viewer because these photographs highlight the injustice. The sense of the Jim Crow laws is then automatically put into question.

Eventually, as already mentioned before, segregation was abolished in many parts by the Civil Rights Act. This also implied the abolition of segregated water fountains.

4.2. Street Fights

Many demonstrations and activities against segregation laws and for civil rights took place in public open spaces, i.e. streets. One of the biggest demonstrations was the non-violent Birmingham Movement in 1963 planned by Martin Luther King. He believed that the South's largest city "could greatly help the civil rights movement" (Dierenfield 80). Due to the city's violence past, King knew that segregationists would try to violently stop the movement in this city so that racist behavior would make the "rest of the world looking [and] compel federal intervention" (80). The opponents involved in this street fights were then black non-violent demonstrators and white violent policemen. This contrast emphasizes the whites' misbehavior and the blacks' attempt to fight for equality and passive resistance. Thanks to photojournalism meaningful snapshots could be presented to the public which exactly fitted to what King wanted. Photographs showing street fights clearly support the image of the innocent black and the violent white. Feelings of guilt can be then transported as the wrongdoing is carried out by the superior group making the black community look even more inferior.

Bill Hudson was the main photographer of the Birmingham Movement. One of his photographs captured "the nightmarish attack on young Walter Gadsden" (Kasher 95) which was published in different newspapers (Fig. 4). They strongly shocked many Americans who then reacted to these photographs, for example by writing emotional letters:

> Now I've seen everything. The news photographer who took that picture of a police dog lunging at a human being has shown us in unmistakable terms how low we have sunk and will surely have awakened a feeling of shame in all who have seen that picture, who have any notion of human dignity. The man is being lunged at was not a criminal being tracked down to prevent his murdering other men; he was, and is, a man. [...] If the United States doesn't stand for some average decent level of human dignity, what does it stand for? (95)

This statement by a Maryland woman unambiguously demonstrate the population's feelings of guilt and shame after knowing about the street fights and violence against young black demonstrators.

Finally, also this movement led to some rapid changes: "In exchange for an end to demonstrations the compromise guaranteed the desegregation of retail facilities and the nondiscriminatory hiring and promoting of black industrial workers" (97). In addition to this change, the movement generally made progress as photography made the government succumb to the activists' constant pressure.

5.   Conclusion: Photojournalism as Initiator of Change

This term paper has shown that during the African-American Civil Rights Movement, photojournalism had a high impact on the American population and the rest of the world. Meaningful photographs by both white and black photographers illustrated the blacks' everyday life and public appearances in a manner which was unknown to the public leading to feelings of empathy and guilt. The increasing number of photographs more and more shocked the public so that, in the end, the US government had to react in order to save face. The blacks' constant pressure and insistence paid out: The Civil Rights Act in 1964 and the Voting Rights Act in 1965 finally improved the blacks' situation in society by giving them the right to vote and the permission to attend public places.

However, one can detect that people of color still face racism today and feel inferior. "Many who believe that America has entered a post-racial period [...] argue that poor blacks suffer from racial inequality due to their living in poverty" (Higginbotham 20). It would therefore be interesting to compare today's photographs of colored people with those of the 1950s and 1960s. This could then illustrate how racism changed in the course of time. While colored people in former times mainly suffered from obvious and visible inequality they nowadays have to endure a "less blatant and more subtle" discrimination which is more difficult to discover. In addition, one could compare the importance of new media for photojournalism. Especially the internet gives photojournalists the opportunity to spread news, photographs and messages easily. But this also demands from the photographer that he or she chooses the 'right' photograph in order to transport his message and avoid publishing an innumerable amount of photographs. This surplus of images is namely already noticeable in the new media since "the camera phone has essentially turned any casual observor [sic!] to a potential photojournalist" (Keller).

6. List of Figures

Fig.1: Bruce Davidson, *The Selma-to-Montgomery March,* 1965. <http://www.nytimes.com/2012/10/28/opinion/sunday/the-price-of-a-black-president.html>.

Fig.2: Gordon Brown, *African American Children Peering into a Whites Only Playground,*1956.
<http://clatl.com/atlanta/ImageArchives?oid=7367694&by=7367679>.

Fig.3:   Eliott Erwitt, *Segregated Water Fountains*, North Carolina, 1950.
<http://www.stephendaitergallery.com/dynamic/artwork_display.asp?ArtworkID=
1255>.

Fig.4: Bill Hudson, *William Gadsden attacked by K-9 units outside 16th Street
Baptist Church,* Birmingham, 1963.
<http://www.pbs.org/thisfar.byfaith/journey_4/p_6.html>.

7. Works Cited

Abel, Elizabeth. *Signs of the Times: The Visual Politics of Jim Crow*. Berkeley: University of California Press, 2010.

Berger, Maurice. "A Radically Prosaic Approach to Civil Rights Images" 24 Mai. <http://lens.blogs.nytimes.com/2012/07/16/a-different-approach-to-civil-rights-images/>.

Cashman, Sean Dennis. *African-Americans and the Quest for Civil Rights, 1900-1990*. New York: NYU Press, 1991.

Cookman, Claude Hubert. *American Photojournalism: Motivations and Meanings*. Evanston: Northwestern University Press, 2009.

Dierenfield, Bruce J. *The Civil Rights Movement*. Edinburgh: Pearson, 2004.

Higginbotham, F. Michael. *Ghosts of Jim Crow: Ending Racism in Post-Racial America*. New York: NYU Press, 2013.

Kasher, Steven. *The Civil Rights Movement. A Photographic History, 1954-68*. New York: Abbeville Press, 2000.

Keller, Jared. "Photojournalism in the Age of New Media." 24 Mai. <http://www.theatlantic.com/technology/archive/2011/04/photojournalism-in-the-age-of-new-media/73083/>.

Lemagny, Jean-Claude and André Rouillé (eds.). *A History of Photography*. Cambridge: Cambridge University Press, 1987.

Ovell, Miles. *American Photography*. Oxford: Oxford University Press, 2003.

Oxford Advanced Learner's Dictionary. 7th edition. Oxford: Oxford UP, 2006.

Roberts, John. *The Art of Interrupting: Realism, Photography and the Everyday*. Manchester: Manchester University Press, 1998.

Smith, Terry. *Making the Modern: Industry, Art, and Design in America*. Chicago: University of Chicago Press, 1994.

Slattery, Karen and Marc Doremus. "Photojournalism: Know Thyself." 24 Mai. 2013 <http://digitaljournalist.org/issue0805/photojournalist-know-thyself.html>.

Tischauser, Leslie V. *Jim Crow Laws*. Santa Barbara, CA: ABC-CLIO, 2012.

Tormey, Jane. *Cities and Photography*. London: Routledge, 2013.

Wallace, Robert. "The Restraints: Open and Hidden." *Life Magazine* 24 Sept. 1956: 98-108.

Lightning Source UK Ltd.
Milton Keynes UK
254211UK00005B/19